Beginnings

Carmel Reilly

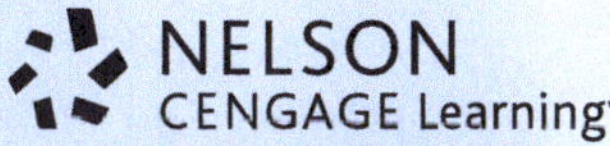

Australia • Brazil • Japan • Korea • Mexico • Singapore • Spain • United Kingdom • United States

Beginnings

Fast Forward
Turquoise Level 18

Text: Carmel Reilly
Illustrations: Jane Wallace-Mitchell (pp.8-13), Liz Alger (pp.14-17) and Julian Bruere (pp.18-23)
Editor: Cameron Macintosh
Design: James Lowe
Series design: James Lowe
Production controller: Seona Galbally
Photo research: Gillian Cardinal
Audio recordings: Juliet Hill, Picture Start
Spoken by: Matthew King and Abbe Holmes
Reprint: Jennifer Foo

Acknowledgements
The author and publisher would like to acknowledge permission to reproduce material from the following sources: Photographs by Photolibrary.com, cover, pp. 4, 5, 7; Photos.com, back cover, p. 6.

ISBN 978 0 17 012639 7
ISBN 978 0 17 012633 5 (set)

Cengage Learning Australia
Level 7, 80 Dorcas Street
South Melbourne, Victoria Australia 3205
Phone: 1300 790 853

Cengage Learning New Zealand
Unit 4B Rosedale Office Park
331 Rosedale Road, Albany, North Shore NZ 0632
Phone: 0508 635 766

For learning solutions, visit cengage.com.au

Printed in Australia by Ligare Pty Ltd
4 5 6 7 8 9 10 21 20 19 18 17

THE UNIVERSITY OF MELBOURNE

Evaluated in independent research by staff from the Department of Language, Literacy and Arts Education at the University of Melbourne.

Beginnings

Carmel Reilly

Contents

Chapter 1

EXPLAINING THE WORLD

All cultures have their own **creation** stories. Some of these stories are very alike, while others are different from each other.

Creation stories are handed down from generation to generation.

What all creation stories have in common is that they explain how the world was made, how things in the world came to be, and why things happen the way they do.

Creation stories from different cultures also explain how life came about.
They tell how animal life, plant life and human life began.

Creation stories help people everywhere to understand the world and their place in the world.

Chapter 2

OUT OF THE DARKNESS

Many creation stories begin with darkness.

In **Persian** stories, the main god, Ahura Mazda, was the creator of all that was good. From the darkness, he made the Sun, the stars, humans, animals and plants.

Although Ahura Mazda was the main god,
he did not have all the power.
There were other gods,
including an evil god who was always trying to destroy
the good things that Ahura Mazda created.

Running Words 169

As well as creating the world and everything in it, like water, earth, and animals, Ahura Mazda also made a man.

Before Ahura Mazda had finished creating everything, the evil god attacked the world and destroyed much in it, including the man.

But this didn't stop Ahura Mazda.
He went right back to work
and made more good things for the world.

Finally, Ahura Mazda made two new humans – a man and a woman.
The man and the woman became the mother and father of the human race.

Although they had been created from good, humans would never be safe from evil, because the evil god had brought it into the world.

From this time on, they would always be open to the forces of evil.

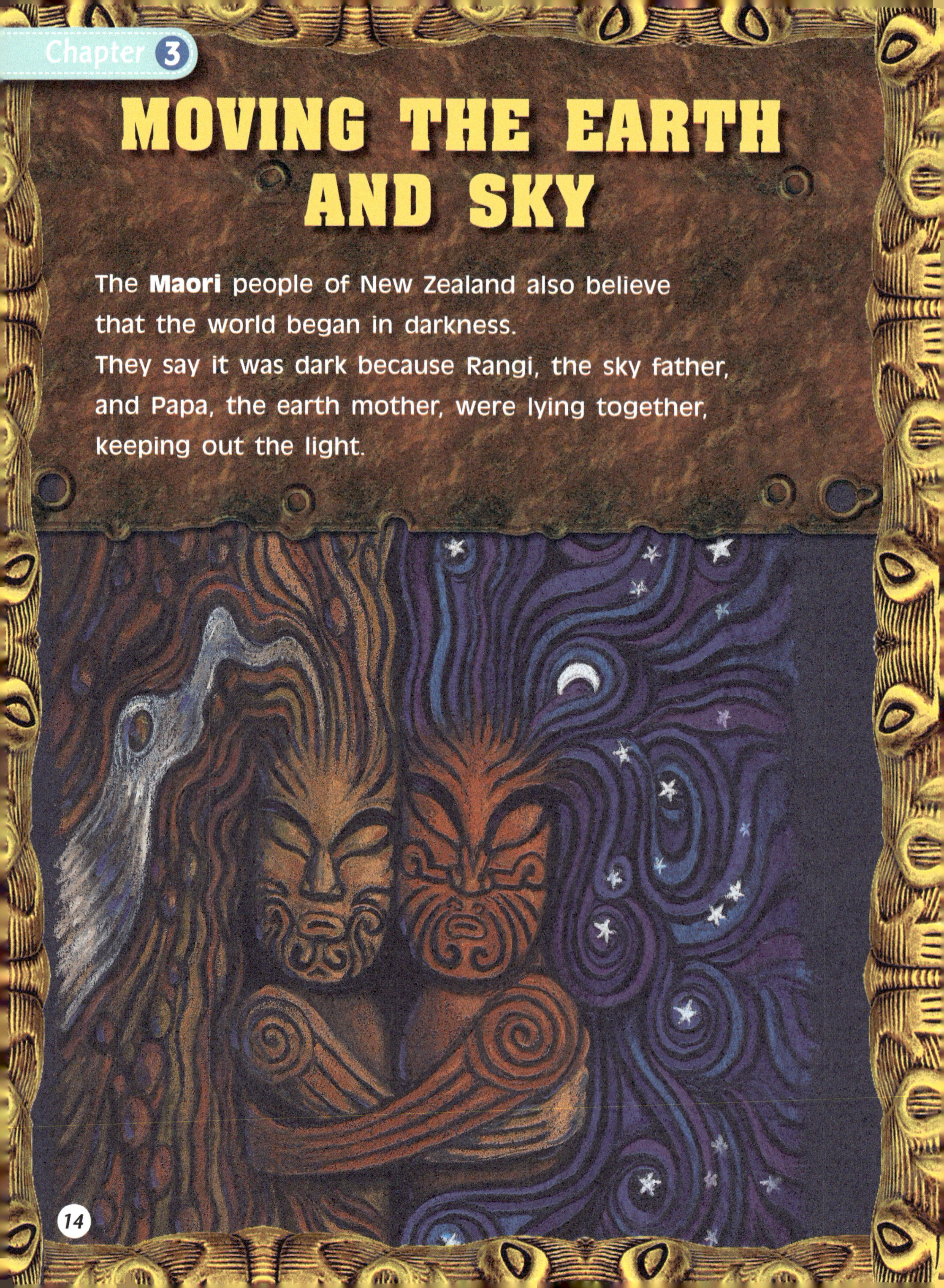

Chapter 3

MOVING THE EARTH AND SKY

The **Maori** people of New Zealand also believe that the world began in darkness.
They say it was dark because Rangi, the sky father, and Papa, the earth mother, were lying together, keeping out the light.

Rangi and Papa had many children who were all gods.
Their children did not like the darkness,
so one of them, Tane, god of the forests,
forced his mother and his father apart.

After this, the sky stayed far above the Earth,
and let the light in.

Later, Tane was living on the Earth.
He decided he needed a wife.
There were no women around, so he made one from sand.
He breathed life into her, and she became the first human.

As Tane breathed life into his wife,
he knew that the breath of life would one day leave her.
So it was that humans were not like gods –
they could not live forever.

Chapter 4

OUT OF THE SEA

The **Mayan** people of **Central America** believed that gods created the world from the sea. After making the land and the plants, the gods thought the world needed more life, so they made animals.

But the animals couldn't speak to the gods.
They could only make noises
that the gods couldn't understand.

As a result, the gods decided to make humans,
who would be more like gods.

First, the gods tried to make humans from mud, but the mud turned into rocks.
Then the gods tried to make humans from wood, but the people were not very intelligent.

Finally, the gods found some yellow, red and black corn, which they ground up and mixed with water. They made this mix into four men and four women and gave them life.

The gods were happy with the corn people,
apart from one thing –
the corn people were too intelligent.

So the gods decided to cloud the people's minds so that the people would never understand everything clearly.
As a result, people would always need the gods to help them with life's problems.

Glossary

Central America the area that joins North and South America, and includes modern-day countries such as Guatemala, Nicaragua and Panama

creation the act of creating something

Maori the native people of New Zealand

Mayan the ancient people of Central America

Persian from ancient or modern Persia (now called Iran)

Index